Council Estate Kid Untold Stories

For Margaret Southin and
Ron Greenall

Chapter 1.

The plight of the English working classes and poor has long been a bone of contention for the ruling classes. From punishment for being poor through to philanthropic and empathetic, at times.

Throughout the middle ages each parish was responsible for its own poor and they were catered for by outdoor and family relief. With the growth of the population and by Tudor times the poor were becoming a problem. Parish poor rates rose and any outsider who looked like they might be poor or need relief such as gypsies were beaten out of the parish by the men with sticks. Parish boundaries were secured and beaten on Saint's Days often resulting in fights with the next parish. Maybe a forerunner of football violence.

Traveller's passing through the parish were often given a meal and lodgings for one night and then moved on. Under the Bloody Code one could get executed for spending times with Gypsies or Egyptians as the Tudor records listed them. The poor were eventually categorised as deserving and undeserving poor [often degraded to vagabonds or sturdy beggars].

Because there was now a poor rate, many tax payers felt aggrieved about paying for the poor. People like single mothers where often carried over the parish boundary in childbirth so that the next parish had to pay for the child and mother. Similarly, women who had children from different men were referred to in Tudor times as Repeaters!

After the Forty Third of Elizabeth the population continued to grow and by the 1830s a new poor law was needed and then amended later in the century. This brought in the introduction of the Work House. A one stop place of incarceration for the poor, ill, mentally ill and often criminals. They were sold off in the Thatcherite style as franchises and the companies that ran them often used the cheapest food and got the poor to do the worst jobs such as Oakum picking and stone breaking in order to maximize profits.

These Benthamite institutions were penopticans with the all seeing eye of God and the wardens watching the poor. Man and Wife, parent and child and male and female were separated off in the silence of the workhouse. The stigma of less eligibility was the theme and even burial was done in the confines of the workhouse with the body being buried in quicklime to burn the bones to nothing. This meant that even the soul cannot be saved on judgement day as there was no body to resurrect.

Private landlords ran slum tenements with many sharing one room and a tap and toilet for the whole street. Cholera was rife. Some companies even paid their workers in tokens so that they had to live in their houses and shop in their shop. Meanwhile, the middle classes had servants and lived away from the workers. It has always baffled me why the working classes want to emulate the middle class. It has always been, know your place and even the Church of England reinforced this with hymns like *All Things Bright and Beautiful,* 'The rich man in his castle, the poor man at his gate'. Even death divided the classes. The most prominent members of society were buried near the church door so that they might be seen by the congregation, every Sunday: or at the East end, nearer God. The poor, if they got a marker [a headstone would cost a year's wages in 1921] were buried fathers away, whilst Criminals and non-Anglicans were buried in the consecrated, un holy, north side.

Philanthropists like Titus Salt built better accommodation for his workers at Saltaire as did Rowntree and Cadbury. The state of the working poor was highlighted in the unhealthiest of the soldiers joining up for the Boer war but the workhouses and slums were still around as late as the 1940s.

During the wars the classes mixed together in the army and by the 1940's it was decided that as a result of Nazi bombing and as a reward to the masses a new National Insurance, Health and housing scheme should be set up to reward the generation who had been subjected to total war. It was the Bevanite government that ejected Churchill from power in 1945 and the building of New Parks Estate in Leicester was began.

My father lived in the Tudor Road area as a child and he says that he can remember Polish Prisoners of War building the new estate which was about a mile north west of the city centre. He can also remember American tanks passing through the area with soldiers sitting upon them. He used to shout 'Give us a gum chum' to them and they would throw sticks of chewing gum.

The houses were built by government design of either pre –formed concrete or iron and concrete build. The better houses and were built of bricks and reserved for the Police and Fire Services and were intermingled in. This shows the initial optimism of the creating of council estates as utopias. All houses had indoor toilets and running water with baths and kitchens. A garden was also planned into the build. Leicester became encircled with council estates for rewards for heroes returning from the war.

To be cynical all the houses looked the same so the stigma of less eligibility was always there. Similarly, the Police got the better brick houses highlighting their heightened status within the class.

The first four houses were occupied in 1946 and a new parish church, St Aiden's was designed by Sir Basil Spence [who had designed the new Coventry Cathedral] and had a copper roof. In 1956 blocks of flats were also built.

New parks was medieval and then Tudor hunting lodge and the word estate conjures up the idea of such a thing. One can understand why the Scots call them, schemes. There is still evidence of medical life in the area, a moated site near Battersbee Road and ridge and furrow barely visible near Western Park. The houses all had decent sized front and rear gardens, ample for playing, relaxing or growing things. Almost a reproduction of the old village houses with their gardens measured in rods and perches, way before land was taken off the poor by the cruel enclosure awards and ring fenced farms.

The houses were rented to the people from the slum areas of Leicester like Wharf Street and My Grandmother moved in from Catherine Street with my Grandfather who had just returned from fighting in Belgium. They had three children. My grandfather, John Thomas Burniston was from Darlington, originally and bizarrely enough when I researched the family tree it transpires that Margaret Cook, the explorer James Cook is a direct ancestor.

My father John Southin or Big Joe, as he was called grew up in the Tudor Road area of the city. His house backed onto the railway lines and he didn't know who his father was. It could have been a butcher from High Street in Leicester who was his mother's first husband. He had a different surname from his brother and sister who were called Palmer after his Mother's new husband John Palmer, a bus driver.

I think that the young John Southin was initially looked after by his Grandmother who had money through the Simpson family as he went to public school. This was not to last as John had a tough upbringing by his step farther and had no Christmas celebrations and left Mantle Road Secondary Modern School at 15 years old. His step father died and his mother married a violent Irish man called Quinn. John beat him for hitting his mother and was kicked out of the house and he moved in with my mother and Grandmother in New Parks after spending a few nights in the Highfields area in a doss house.

My Dad's life had been tough and he began working as a gas fitter for British Gas. As an apprentice he went everywhere on his bike, all over Leicestershire in all weathers. After successfully completing his apprenticeship he changed vocation to become a fireman.

He won awards for bravery, but was always injured. He ran into a building in Leicester with his hose holding the brass nozzle and hit the electric junction box making him blind for a month! He soon became a fire engine driver and he was moved to the old Victorian Fire Station off Green Lane Road. It was during this period that he started a second job as an undertaker. He was sent to Abbwfan in Wales where there was a landslide that took the lives of the primary school children and staff. I think that this haunted him for the rest of his life and had post-traumatic stress disorder. Over the years this led to agoraphobia and the only way to combat that was to drink, which ultimately led to alcoholism. Some of my earliest memories of my father was him being injected into his back side on the sofa by a doctor to keep him alive. That period was dark with him going into The Carlton Hayes Hospital to dry out. It was a simple choice between death and being there for his 6 year old son. He chose to survive and live another 13 years.

Chapter 2.

The optimism of the council estate by the 1960s and 70s had changed. The stigma was back. In The Who's film *Quadrophenia* ,that was released in 1978 has a line that the main character Jimmy spits out in derision towards rockers 'long hair and dirty clobber, estates and third class tickets'.

During the 60s and 70s most families on the estate were respectable working families. Because, most were of the Baby Boomer Generation most had given birth to the X Generation and had young families of the ages of 5 through to 16. These children went through the new comprehensive system.

New Parks House Primary School was a red brick school standing in its own playing field. It had an air raid siren on the roof which was tested every now and again, for the cold war. The quality of education was good and strict. There was a good camaraderie between the lads on the estate and every weekends there were jumpers for goalposts on the greens. Some streets even set up their own football teams.

Unlike Saltaire there were pubs provided for the community. The Good Neighbours [always good for a punch up], The Rocket [where my Father drank], The Shoemakers and The Triangles. All soulless, building that were like the houses, functional and Bauhaus angular. For a treat as a child on a summer's evening my Dad would drink drive us in his Hillman Avenger to the Nag's Head Pub in Glenfield, where I could sit in the pub garden and drink bottled Vimto through a soggy paper straw. The first of the supermarkets was being built beyond the pub garden, by the CO-OP.

Violence was not just confined to the Good Neighbours. The estate became a place where men and boys sorted their own problems out. Most the lads that I played with were a year or two older than me. I often had to prove my standing by fighting and once I hit a lad with a metal spade in the head as he walked past my house. I was 7 or 8 years old! My Dad was an extremely strong man who thought that work equalled pain. He could dig 12 double graves all over Leicestershire in a shift. He was a quiet man but if he was provoked or upset he was a nightmare and would squeeze people's throats to breaking point. Our house was never robbed and trouble never came to our door thanks to Big Joe.

I did get onto trouble as an 8 or 9 year old child. The older lads, The Mephams, Richards and Drivers took me to a house and asked me to keep watch whilst they went in. I had no idea that they were burgluring in! I thought the house was empty and it was a games. The Police came and took me home. I was warned but nothing came of it. The Police could be dodgy. When I was 13 or 14 I went fishing on my bike to Wanlip, with Nick Martin, which is about about 15 miles away. It was October and getting dark, Nick's bike had a flat and his Dad came and took him home. I had to cycle home in the dark alone, with no lights. In Beaumont Leys two coppers stopped me for riding on the pavement and gave me a warning telling me to walk the final 5 miles and not ride!

We went everywhere on our bikes. I can remember one early morning, riding along Blackbird Road with Neil Cank and Wayne Smith, going fishing again on a Sunday morning. I would be 13 years old. We road behind a workman going to work on his bike. Wayne road past him and made a motorbike noise. The guy grabbed Wayne around the neck and punched him!

The kids on the estate made their own fun. Building dens in the bushes near the school, making go-carts and racing them or space hopper races with privet hedge jumps. Everyone was football crazy. One kid called Vincent was so poor that his only shoes were wellies. He used to play football in them, went to school in them and even wore them with shorts in the summer. He was surprisingly good at football in these wellies and a good right winger. I'm surprised Gary Lineker didn't wear a pair.

The traditional yearly festivities are always depicted by the media in the countryside with the changes in the seasons. On the estate certain seasons were iconic. The summertime especially the hot summer of 1976 consisted of water fights with the neighbours kids, soaked to the skin with soggy clothes. Sharpening lolly sticks into knives on the concrete.

Ice creams from the oakey bloke with lolly's such as Cider Barrel, FAB, Funny feet and the horrible but cheap Mini Milks. Jubbly's which were triangular flavoured ice and the new Slush Puppies.

Kids played Kerby which was a game that required a thrown football to hit the corner of the kerb and bounce back for a point. If one caught it, two points. Caledine Road seemed like the mighty River Ouse back then, but as an adult it was 5 yards across. Magnifying glasses burnt holes in paper and insects. There was a hippy woman a few doors up from our house. My mother called her Loopy but her real name was Eileen. She liked a drink and during the summer music blared out of her windows in the afternoons as she drank in the garden. Everyone was fed up of her playing Dexy's Midnight Runners! Nights would often be spent with her arguing and fighting with her bloke and the arrival of the Police.

It's amazing how quickly autumn follows summer and the immediate change in weather from August to September. No one celebrated Halloween in the 1970s and 80s on the estate but Bonfire Night was a whole different matter. Having said that, I can remember standing on the fungus ridden felled tree trunk in the yard at New Parks House Primary School and looking for witches flying in the air in the afternoon autumn sun. Similarly, The Jepson twins would dress up as witches and wave out of their windows. Wayne Beazeley and myself did make pumpkins out of baking potatoes with birthday candles insides.

From mid-October wood would be collected by the kids and piled onto greens and wasteland to make huge bonfires. Children would go door to door asking for wood for the bonnie. Wooden garden gates were stolen and my Dad secured out gate to the concrete post with wire! The bonfires would be often lit before bonfire night and had to be rebuilt.

Penny for the Guy was another big thing and my Mam made me a good Guy out of old clothes and I sat either outside of my front gate or outside the shops on Aikman Avenue with it. Thursdays were a good day as the council workmen from the depot on Caledine Road had just been paid and felt flush and generous.

Bonfire Night was a crazy night. Bonfires raged on every green like a mad Pagan festival. Every house seemed to have their own fireworks made by Standard Fireworks. They started going off at 4pm and lasted until about Midnight. The sky was heavy with smoke and the sound of fire engine sirens and blue lights flickering through the darkness.

My Dad always let the fireworks off. He kept them in a biscuit tin. If I was good he would often let one off on a Saturday afternoon beforehand. My Mam would make hot dogs and onions and jacket spuds.

From the start of December the estate would be a city of lights. It's amazing to think that those who hold Christmas dear to their hearts are often the poorest. Fairy lights, fake snow on windows and model Santa's were everywhere. Middle Class people though it was crass but it is magical that people make the effort. One house on New Parks Boulevard actually had a full sized Santa that was tied to his chimney and illuminated by a security light. The lights and decorations were so exciting that as a small boy my mother would ask me to count the trees on the way back from town on the 96 Midland Red bus. The first tree was always in the window of the mower people Oswald Cox on Sanvey Gate. The build up to Christmas would be so exiting I can remember riding all the way to Groby with Lloyd Harding on his Grifter looking at decorations. It's amazing he got anywhere on his Grifter it weighed a ton and had 3 twist grip colour coded gears but the middle gear was a slip gear for some reason.

The Fire Brigade would come around the streets playing loud Christmas songs and dressed a fireman up as Father Christmas in a motorised sleigh. My Mother would take me to visit Santa at the big CO-OP department store on High Street in Leicester but, every year Santa did scale the Lewis' Department store tower. Our house was decorated inside with a tinsel tree [fire hazard], balloons stick to the polystyrene tiles in the ceiling [fire hazard], fairy lights around the fire place and cards blue tacked to the wall. There were also plastic coated hanging garlands and baubles from the ceiling [fire hazard].

Summer holidays for the estate was centred on the July Fortnight what was when the factories closed down for two weeks? Big Hoirsery Company's like Pex and shoe companies like British Shoe Corporation would spew out their workers for 2 weeks. Skegness, Mablethorpe and Great Yarmouth were the most popular destinations. We did not have much money so we went on mystery trips for the day run by British Rail and you could end up anywhere. Firstly it was the old cabin carriage with pub carpet seats that stunk of stale smoke. Later it was the Formica tabled open plan coaches.

Chapter 3

Summer holidays on the estate were six to eight weeks long ending in the Abbey Park Show? The City of Leicester show that was a bit like a County Show. The kids on the estate spent the summers mostly playing football on the greens with very few families going on holidays.

My first proper holidays were to Butlin's in Skegness, staying in ex-army or air force chalets on iron bunkbeds! Eating was in huge halls regulated by colour coded times. 'You vill enjoy yourselves!'

As the 80's progressed more and more people dribbled abroad and my first visit to Majorca was with the more affluent Simon Ward's family. My mind was expanded beyond belief with the change of culture and that was my desire to travel and escape the estate.

It was so beautiful, the sea was turquoise, I'd only seen the sea a couple of times coming from Leicester. The sea was always grey at Skegness. There were mountains and once again coming from Leicester in the Midland's Plain there are none. The fresh fruit and vegetables were nothing like the paltry things one got in the COOP in Aikman Avenue.

New Parks was well town planned and had good access to all amenities and transport links. There were no dark , 'mugger's alleys', and there were large green recreational areas. The Secondary school had a huge playing field that led onto the huge Western Park and was an awesome area for the estate giving it freedom to breathe.

The city was now encircled by huge council estates. Beaumont Leys had a discoloured yellow grass possibly because all the sewage and waste was pumped there in late Victorian times from the city and the steam powercd Abbey pumping station. There were new developments to the east of Leicester but they were often tagged onto or into existing or cleared Victorian housing. These areas were planned differently. Included tower blocks or planned by Dysart on the European models and were full of 'mugger's alleys'. These estates won awards and spread across the country with schemes such as The Byker Wall. As Paul Weller wrote, 'The planner's dream went wrong'.

The education system in Leicester was single gender and not co-eduational. This worked very well but was a strain on the council's budget having double the amount of schools. New Parks Boys' School was a truly comprehensive school set up with 1950s grammar school values. The catchment included the estate and the affluent middle class area of Glenfield Road, Letchworth Road as well as Newfoundpool's terraced streets.

Braunstone Frith was within the catchment of the newly relocated Alderman Newton's School next door, which was a public school in the city centre but was a comprehensive now. The boys' school was built on tradition and the wooden panelled entrance hall was full of trophies and photographs of the school's rugby, football and cricket teams.

The pastoral system was divided into five forms and houses, Bannister, Cheshire, Whittle, Hilary and Scott. There was great inter- house and inter- form rivalry and sport competitions. The teachers were mostly fair but very firm and there were shouts of 'You Boy!' echoing down the corridors like a Pink Floyd voice on The Wall.

If one kept their head down and complied you got through. But if you were a good sportsman you progressed. However, if you did not comply in any way you were punitively caned, beaten or embarrassed. Mr King hit you with his shoe that had a chalk number written in reverse on the sole! The school teams won county cups year after year and there was a great pride of the school that was lost through almalgamisation then the awful process of acadamisation.

Strange things happened in the school that could never happen nowadays because of safeguarding. Kids could go home for lunch! Some kids went to the shops and bought cobs and stuffed them full of Walker's Crisps. A dog would occasionally get into the school and cause chaos and occasionally there was an intruder.

Jaffa was one such intruder. He lived in the flats near the school and some students would taunt him by shouting 'Jaffa' outside his flat. Jaffa would then chase the kids with his walking stick. The poor chap once followed the kids into the school changing rooms and held them hostage and even the teachers had problems reasoning with him.

Teaching was good within the school and the lessons were well taught and controlled. The books were always marked and the staff had a genuine concern for the students. The teaching may have been text book, chalk and talk and work sheet led but it worked. School trips to The Lake District, Narrow Boating and Paris gave the students a chance to escape the estate and extend their horizons. The teachers would go to the pub in the evenings through. The teacher's strikes of the 1980s was a start to the death knell in the goodwill between teachers and the government and Saturday morning sports fixtures stopped. This was a golden age of teaching, with respect towards the staff and system.

Somewhere during New Labour things changed to schools becoming businesses, sold off to academies. Entering the career was made easier for cheaper, younger, less educated teachers. Academia was replaced by industry and cost and teachers were capabilitied out. Schools became less the focal point or respected institution of the area.

It was amazing how with school uniforms kids managed to be fashionable. Looking back through school photographs one can see the long haired, Grebo lads and the skinheads of the late 1970s and early 80s. Kipper ties of the 70's and the flick haired lads of the 1980s with their ties done so it was a thin tie rather than the thicker end.

1. Council estate fashion was far cooler than those emanating from the fashion houses. They are linked as bizarrely enough the working classes emulate middle and upper class style. Barbour, Burberry, Aquascutum, Lyle and Scott, Pringle! However, the upper classes wear labels without showing them unlike the crassness of the newly wealthy peasants.

Youth culture came up from the streets and every kid, had to belong. As a younger lad I can remember looking up to the older lads and wanting to be like them and go into town on the bus without being with my mother! The youth cultures fought each other and their identity was a badge. Estates fought estates, schools fought schools, and football team's fans fought other fans. It's just how it was. Probably dating back to Saints' days and Lords of misrule from the middle ages, it was the depth of understanding and attention to detail that was important in youth cultures. All had to be coded and to a certain extent be underground and when it became commercial it became blaze and worthless. Nowadays Primark fashion and people wearing Ramones T-shirts who have never even heard of them is as ridiculous as the awful branded Gucci and emblazoned D and G clothing.

When the fun fair came to Western Park there were the traditional fights on the park every night between New Parks and Braunstone estates. I was a Mod during the 80s Mod revival and I can remember Skinheads wanting to fight me because of that. I was also chased down Welford Road by Chelsea football casuals because I was a mod. When I was a casual I was chased by Chelsea Casuals because I was a Leicester Casual.

If you were a Grebo you grew your hair long, wore your bands t shirts and wore jeans and leather. Mods and Skin heads had their codes often documented by authors such as Richard Barnes or through tradition. There were Punks, New Romantics, Trendies, Townies, Psych Billies, Teds, and Casuals to name a few. All had their own music, haircuts and even places that they socialised in. The Demontfort Pub in Leicester was a bikers bar for example and The Pinch of Snuff was the casuals pub. The youth of the estate naturally ventured into the city to drink, when that age came unlike those from villages and small towns who tended to stay within the village or small town pub scene. It wasn't just estates that could be violent places villages like Anstey in Leicestershire and Louth in Lincolnshire were hard places and these existed all over the country, Winlaton in Gateshead and Newbiggin by the Sea in Northumberland to name a few.

Chapter 4

It's not so strange that a society that was so obsessed with being classified into distinct groups with such rivalry should squabble about the class system. Working class people wanting to be middle class and middle class wanting to be upper class. Each class has stereotyped views of the other. Mr Kent told me at school during my sixth form mock interview that 'It was best that I didn't put New Parks Estate on my applications'. He was not being snobbish but looking out for my best interests in a stereo typed way.

The main people who dislike the working class tend to be those who have left the estate for a private house on a private building estate. They look down their noses at where they have come from.

The class system is based on many things such as university education, the area one lives, the profession of one's parents the music and fashion one follows. It is deeply rooted and difficult to change class.

For example, the Beckhams might have millions of Pounds and a stately pile. However, they are still middle class through the clothes that they wear, the R and B Music they listen to, their tattoos to name but a few things that link them to their original class. However, with easier access to university and salaries some think that they are middle class. In Tudor times these newly landed, Jonny come lately, noveux riche types were just as deluded and disliked but without the jet skis, Audis on bubble payments and crass labels.

Margaret Thatcher and the greedy 80s and to a certain extent 90s got their history very wrong. Just as many periods look back to a golden age, Thatcher was very much a Whiggish idealist. Privatisation was a key idea. An Englishman's home is his castle. However, this Victorian idea did not rely upon borrowing and credit and our Victorian forefathers would turn in their graves at the thought of hire purchase and credit cards.

Thatcher sold off the council houses in the Right to Buy Scheme and in some ways returned England to the housing shortages and sync areas of the turn of the century. A lot of right to buyers sold on to make profits and moved away. Social housing went back into the hands of those who wanted to make profits such as private landlords.

The council estate became its long period of decline, a 70 year social experiment for the good of the working classes. I'm not sure if there is a community or it's the myth of community but now with no council control, the estates have become largely private landlords or areas of cheaper housing and have huge social problems such as tab or cigarette houses and drugs. The schools are academies and struggle under private ownership and many stink of lower expectations with careerist teachers.

Chapter 5

Relationships on council estates are not the stereotyped *Little Britain* teenage pregnancy that one might think. In England, culturally the average age of marriage has been 29 for many centuries. This is because a new family unit becomes when a man and woman have their own house and with apprenticeships and saving it was the earliest practicable time. In Japan the male can be 15 years older than the female but in England the age difference is usually around a year or two.

With there being a non-co-educational system, the kids met the opposite gender at places such a Granby Halls in Leicester which held a roller disco on Saturday afternoons. Relationships could also be acquired on the park or near the shops in the summer. When the schools were amalgamated dating became much simpler. Many of my peers started dating at the same time in the 4th and 5th year and I can remember sitting on the same kerb that Gary Heathcote and myself played kerby on as young boys in year 7 and trading stories about our girlfriends and conquests. Loving in box rooms and school playing fields. Kissing on the park and street corners.

Relationships rarely occurred between different social classes and one finds that areas that dislike or have rivalries with each other have very little cross relationships. This too can be traced back to parish boundaries and medieval times.

There are very few romantic relationships between; New Parks and Braunstone, Leicester and Nottingham for example. The inter marriage between rival settlements is quite rare throughout England and there is an interesting study done upon Robin Hood's Bay on the Eastern Coast of England highlighting this.

Political lines are now blurred in traditional Labour strongholds dominated by the estate. As a child Greville Janner would come around the streets in his car waving and asking for votes. He visited my primary school and showed Gary Heathcote and myself his magic ball trick [something it turns out he did in other ways]. Janner and his father held Leicester West as a safe Labour seat. However, as the result in Blyth in the 2019 Christmas election has shown the estates have no loyalty to Labour anymore and it is with speculation that the working classes are now confused where the boundaries and lines are anymore. Is it media or is it real life and changes that have altered many things as we enter a new decade in 2020?

Chapter 6

Many things have changed over the past 40 years that have altered both the working classes and the council estate. When I left school in 1987, I only knew two people out of both my school year and Alderman Newton's School that went to university. Now as a teacher in 2019 at least a third of the working class students aspire or do go to university. Of course, there are reasons behind this due to funding and accessibility but, this blurs class boundaries to many. In a period when credit and mortgages are harder to get, more and more people now rely upon renting and the safety net of the respectable social housing of the council estate has all but gone. This book is not a Marxist look at social housing it is aimed to be as unbiased as politically possible by someone who grew up on an estate. I set out to be revisionist in a *Hodge and his Masters* style. The strange thing is that council estates have not grown and continued in a morphology spread. Instead new housing developments were made separately and not tagged on. Schools might have sold their playing fields but the council estate school fields are rarely bought.

The media has made us into a generation of nondeferred gratification and upwardly mobile peasants who think that our station deserves an Audi, Mercedes or BMW that only our masters could once own. We too can have the four bedroomed, detached home that we haven't had to work too hard for. There's no need for the council estate for its intended audience or is there?

I was pleased when my 80 year old mother left her house on the estate and moved into a bungalow near me. I had become afraid of the people around her. The families that she had known all of her life had moved away. The Police helicopter was always circling and she was threatened by thuggish middle aged neighbours. I do hope that the post war dream does resurrect itself into something positive. As many immigrants from Eastern Europe move into the area it is a new hope, a new community, just as the Indian immigrants after the war revitalised the working class districts of Melton Road.

It is fair to say that the working classes generally own the new technology first, even though they are the poorest. When Sky television first appeared, it was on a six month trial. Stephenson's Drive became known as satellite alley as every house had a white satellite dish attached to its wall. Seven months later all that was left was the rusting frames screwed into the walls!

Doreen next door were the first family that I knew, that had a video player. It was a top loading thing that shook the whole house when it sprang up. The remote control was on a two foot lead and when it fast forwarded the whizzing noise was like a jet taking off.

Gary Heathcote's Nan was the first person that had a sandwich toaster around the area. We called it a Breville. We used to go home from school every lunch and try a different sandwich. Burning our mouths on jam Brevilles or bean Brevilles. There was only one supermarket in the 1980s and that was the COOP Glenfield Superstore. Consequently, unless you wanted to carry bags on the bus and around Leicester City centre, one shopped local.

The Aikman Avenue shops served the estate. There was a COOP, a bakers [Coombs], a shoe shop, newsagent, Boots Chemist, greengrocers and a pet shop. Food was quite basic and fast food was Findus Crispy Pancakes or Vesta Curries. I thought Spaghetti came out of a tin with tomato sauce.

Chapter 7

Like the school, originally the estate was comprehensive. Before the 1980's it was quite difficult to get a mortgage as a large deposit was required. A council house was a good option. The rent on a council house was as much as the repayments on a mortgage so people had to work hard and all professions were found on the estate. Police and Fireman's houses were built into the estate. They did not share the same less eligibility as they were made from brick and not preformed concrete.

My Father told me that when I went to secondary school that I'd meet a lifelong friend. This was true. Mark Vickers was a tall, athletic lad, who was into rugby, like me. However, he was from the middle class, private houses on Glenfield Road. His dad was an accountant. It opened up a new world to me. Their house was nice, it even had a snooker table in the spare room. Some of the lads that I had hung around with on the estate even slept in sleeping bags because their families could not afford quilts. Conversely, Mark's bedroom was en suite!

Mark's Grandpa lived on a farm at Groby and we used to go and stay with him. I'd never really gone into the countryside before and it was freighting at night as there were no street lights and it was so dark that I couldn't see my hand in front of my face. It was such a release for me from the estate. Bradgate Park was close by, Leicester's Lake District.

Mark's Grandpa also took us to play rugby in his Morris 1000 car. He got us to play on Sundays for Belgrave RFC and then Westleigh RFC once again escaping the estate.

My wife comes from a council estate, in Northumberland but, it is part of a small town. Similarly, she speaks of some teachers trying to make a difference and show her new things like bringing in Olives to try as a new food. She was desperate to escape her environment and left as soon as she could for Manchester University. However, there is a big difference in that most of her peers never left the town. In New Park's because it was only a mile from a big city I never saw most of my peers after the last day of school.

Chapter 7

The myth of community is evident in the point that the government have felt it necessary to introduce British Values to schools and the workplace.

Fundamental British Values are not exclusive to being British and are shared by other democratic countries as a way of creating an orderly society, where individual members can feel safe, valued and can contribute for the good of themselves and others.

These will mirror the principles and values of Total People and all the work areas that we support. These will occur throughout your programme and will be promoted by the staff with whom you come into contact.

Democracy

A culture built upon freedom and equality, where everyone is aware of their rights and responsibilities.

Examples

- Leadership and accountability
- Joint decision making
- Team meetings
- The right to protest and petition
- Receiving and giving feedback

Rule of Law

The need for rules to make a happy, safe and secure environment to live and work.

Examples

- Legislation
- Agreed ways of working, policies and procedures
- How the law protects you and others
- Codes of conduct

Respect and Tolerance

Understanding that we all don't share the same beliefs and values. Respecting the values, ideas and beliefs of others whilst not imposing our own others.

Examples

- Embracing diversity
- The importance of religion, traditions, cultural heritage and preferences
- Tackling stereotyping, labeling, prejudice and discrimination

Individual Liberty

Protection of your rights and the right of others you work with.

Examples

- Equality and Human Rights
- Personal Development
- Respect and Dignity
- Rights, choice, consent and individuality

- Values and principles

Council estates were built to promote community, and community centres were added along with other public amenity buildings. However, the estates in Leicester have remained largely, white and working class. Areas of Leicester have become racially lined, for example, Highfields has since the 1960's been largely West Indian and Pakistani, whereas the Melton Road area is largely Indian and Hindu.

Leicester is mostly harmonious in terms of racial relations. The Indian community that settled in Leicester after the partition of the 1940s revitalized the hosiery trade and integrated into the city life, despite living in a distinct area. I have witnessed very little racial tension or racism in Leicester despite it being 40% Asian.

Conversely, Wholly white communities like Hylton Castle in Sunderland, Blyth and Ashington in Northumberland have very strong links to far right groups and very racist views. All these communities voted for Brexit because of immigration, even though there are no immigrants in the area and their local economies are reliant on European Community grants and money.

Culture is a collection of facets; occupation, language, music, fashion, education, family size, traditions, food, arts, etcetera. One can break these down into the class structure, for example middle classes go to the theatre and working classes largely will go to the cinema, in the basic of comparisons.

However, being part of this culture does not mean that one is part of a community as the need to introduce British Values indicates. The government have become worried before about working class values and introduced a subject called Citizenship back in the reign of New Labour but after a huge push and focus by OFSTED, it was shelved as a failure.

Chapter 8

I have always felt a shame of being working class. Not a shame of that I want to be Middle Class, but a shame that I feel is imposed by the Middle Class and the privileged.

I have various examples of this shame. I always felt that I was not worthy when I worked in Leicester University Library, as if I was not meant to be there for some reason.

I had a girlfriend who lived in a huge detached house in Yorkshire and her father was a rich surveyor. When her mother came to my mother's house in New Parks I felt apprehensive and a lowly, not worthy mood, despite my Mother having a lovely home.

The real question is why did I feel like this? Also whom and why was I made to feel like this? Was it some sort of subvert control by the classes above? I was never directly told that I was part of an Ouviere sub class, so how had I learnt this?

I'm not sure if it is a legacy of the shame of less eligibility and the workhouse days of Victorian England that had worked its way into the psyche of the working class or it was through observations of visiting friends private houses in Glenfield and Letchworth Road and comparing those to mine or houses of friends that I'd been in on my estate?

Was it the media or music such as listening to *Saturdays Kids* by The Jam or *Common People* by Pulp. I certainly was not taught it at school. The Teachers at New Parks Boys' School I felt truly wanted the best for the students and the Comprehensive schools of the 70s and 80s were ran along the blue print of the old grammar schools in most cases.

There was no lesser expectations by the teaching staff. The first time that I did see lesser expectations and a pseudo middle class attitude towards the kids was by the new younger breed of teachers that I encountered when I worked in Ashington. Some called the students skip rats behind their backs! I found a similar derisory tone of some of the staff when I taught in South Sunderland. There was a South African deputy head teacher who was absolutely horrible about the students' backgrounds and almost spat out her derision, but she bizarrely wanted the best for them [or her own progress, through a results driven and often cheating environment].

Chapter 9

Working Class culture on the estate was both positive and negative. There were some fashions and behaviors which were self-destructive. For example, the white working class Charva in the North East who listens to the drug related and often racist music New Monkey.

Similarly, whilst the fashion was originally based upon the music and style of the Windrush immigrants of the 1960s, the Skinhead movement and working class fashion was meant to reflect pride and self-worth in the working class but it built into an underclass, negative and often racist scene.

Sport was something positive and many gifted footballers come from the council estates. Some academised schools like the Emmanuel Foundation, sneer at this working class sport and even though they own some schools in council estate areas, they only allow Rugby as it is character building and traditionally middle class.

I still believe that changing class is impossible, it is something that one is born into. Class as aforementioned is culturally based and only by changing the whole of one's culture and not just having more money or a house in a middle class area will still not make a working class person, middle class.

The nouveaux riche or Johnny Come Latelies often display crassness in a desire to change class. Big visible labels on clothing and German cars for example. They feel the need to pretend to be middle class and openly spit derision upon the environment that they hailed from. However, their culture is so ingrained that they cannot escape from their class and neither can their children. It is nurture.

The higher political elite are still privileged and have been educated at the finest schools. During the period of New Labour, Tony Blair actually pretended to be working class and invited icons of the working class and Britpop era to Downing Street. Of course, it was a spin doctor stunt and the likes of Noel Gallagher soon recognized his mistake of buying into this.

Music or popular music can be a social commentary of the working class. Jonny Marr once said that the only way out of Manchester for a working class lad was 'either through music or football'.

I was average at school, but went to study A/Levels before dropping out after a year. I then entered and drifted through many working class jobs. A sales assistant, working in a dairy, being a milk man before wanting a desire for knowledge.

I was working at minus 30 degrees picking boxes in a freezer warehouse and one day thought, I want to go to university. After much research I enrolled with the Open University and after 9 years of working full time in hard manual jobs and studying at the Open University, University of Leicester and University of Nottingham, I finally emerged with two degrees and a Post Graduate Certificate in Education. I still felt that I was a charlatan and should not be this well-educated and I even was accepted and began a PhD at de Montfort University. But the stigma still hangs over me.

Over the years various colleagues have commented. Some positively, saying how they respected me and my knowledge and others who tended to be pseudo middle class, sneering at my vocation, even though I had much higher qualifications.

Chapter 10

I don't believe that in the 21st Century that the middle classes deliberately intend to keep the working class in their position, like the fear of the Victorian Malthusians who wanted to reduce the surplus population. By transportation to the colonies or workhouses.

The working classes are their own restrictors. In an era swamped by the media. The television, social media, magazines, all tell us what we should own and aspire to. Hire purchase, bubble payments, credit cards allow non gratification and enables people to own things that were once only the domain of the upper classes.

However, this entitlement is short lived and theses luxuries are often disappointments. When I was a child I looked up to the older kids who went into town and night clubs. When it was my turn, this was a great disappointment, this analogy was also true when I owned a Tag Heur watch and a Porsche 944! I could be described as a French Socialist at times, but I never look down upon my roots or fear going back to them. I like nice things and often have a Champagne taste on a beer budget but I don't feel entitled to live in a certain area or own certain things to prove my position.

The post war dream of the Labour government was truly forward thinking, utopian and philanthropic. The National Health Service, National Insurance, Education Acts and Council Housing. Its intentions were for a fairer society. Of course, the middle and upper classes moaned because they had to pay more in taxes for the poorer and often vulnerable members of society. Because of the class system deeply entrenched in England there could never be a Volksgemeinschaft.

Being part of a European community and the demise of the Empire. A rise in population, austerity and credit, the future of social housing and the working classes is a difficult one to predict. Social media, privately owned education and bombarded by capitalism and what one should achieve is a million miles away from Samuel Smiles book *Self Help*.

I am not futile enough to think that someone needs to be a decision maker. For example, the Russian Communist example after 1917/18 was unworkable, no marriages as it's sexist, no schools as they just make workers etcetera. I am not convinced that in the 20th and 21st Century the middle classes try to keep the proletariat down in England at all. In fact universities make it much easier for those from working class backgrounds to gain entry.

However, I don't think that there will ever be a working class community that existed in the post war utopian dream. My mother has photographs of a huge street party in Caledine Road in New Parks for the Queen's coronation in the 1950s. Massive tables down the middle of the road and bunting across the road from house to house. Similarly, the Pitman Painters of Ashington highlight some sort of community as does the leek shows and miner's galas.

Alongside class runs immigration and race. I can't understand how Englishmen can be racist or dislike immigration as we are all immigrants. What's a true Englishman look like? Blonde? Brown? Ginger? Englishmen are all mixed race.

Celts, Roman invasion, Angles and Saxons from Germany, Vikings, Normans and all the different countries of the British Empire that came to their motherland, Jamaicans, Africans, Indians, Pakistanis, Yemanis, to name but a few all inter- breeding, inter mingling with the working class and making a stronger, economic nation. Will there be a community or is it a myth? A suitable epilogue would be the fact that the most common archeological find in Medieval deserted villages in England arc keys and studs to reinforce doors. Was there ever a community?

Printed in Great Britain
by Amazon

65244480R00035